Through the Spectrum: 21 Days of Life, Love, Parenthood, and Disabilities

Kris McElroy

BookLeaf Publishing

India | USA | UK

Presentation by *BookLeaf Publishing*

Web: www.bookleafpub.com

E-mail: info@bookleafpub.com

ISBN: 9789358737851

First edition 2023

For my wife Sonya.

For my daughter, Kenzy.

For my bonus daughter, Tejah.

For all of those who feel different from the majority and are trying to find their way.

The Question

I am the vision of my mother and father.
I am a linked vision of my ancestors.
I am a vision broken down as each path turned a
different direction.
I am all the things envisioned for me, yet
deformed from the original piece.
Always battling the question:
WHO AM I?
Everyone has an opinion.
Yet, I keep swirling around the question in my
head unable to find a stable answer.
So, it just leaves me to come back to the
beginning.
The beginning that reminds me,
I am still discovering who I am.

The Journey

My child,
There will be so many messages of who you
should be.
Opinions about who and what you are.
Sometimes they will be so loud that you might
get lost.
But, always find your way back to the center.
The center of you.
Your anchor that will remind you of your power.
The power of your voice.
The power of your whole being.
Throughout every phase of the lifelong journey
discovering who you are.
That journey is a scared gift.
Don't let anyone take it from you.
It is a gift written just for you.

Should I?

Should I take a chance,
a leap of faith,
a tip toe into the unknown,
a plunge into hope,
a climb into healing,
Should I?

I am a trauma survivor.
I have significant mental health conditions.
I am autistic.
I have a neuromuscular and autoimmune
disease.
I am a dad.
I am a husband.
I am an award winning athlete.
I am an artist.
I am transgender.
I am queer.
I am ME.

Should I take a chance at my dreams?
Should I believe I am worthy of love?
Should I advocate for my right to a full life?

Should I push my limits to continue discovering
my true abilities beyond the boxes society has
placed me in?
Should I?
Do you know what I mean?

You

As you walk past the mirror trying not to gaze
too much at what you see as the inner voices
have almost all but filled up the space I want to
remind you - I am here.

You are me.
I am you.
I see you through the dense fog when you are
trying to find your way.
I hear you through the silence of the anxiety that
quiets your voice.
I hold you through the barriers formed by
trauma that make you feel safe.
I taste the sweet hope on your lips that holds
your heart and helps guide the way.

You are me.
I am you.
I will work to calm the inner voices as you work
to continue moving forward as we work together
toward healing.

How Much Can A Body Hold?

Daily stress weighs down the shoulders
Changing the length of the spine over time.

Inflamed fluid-filled joints,
Spastic limbs,
Painful muscles,
Still not responding to any of the doctor's
treatments.

Tattoos cover the scars of self-injury
Some now decades old
With hopes of sharing a new message
That helps when the voices and urges return.

Memories of experiences of the past I'd rather
forget.
Held on like a scorebook across the body.
Coming out when triggered, or with a scent, a
place, a smell, many things.

Itchy, tight fabric clings to my skin.
Ear-piercing sounds fill the air even when no
sound is actually there.
Roller coaster temperatures without my consent.

Constant sensory overload.

How much can a body hold?

Sense of Wonder

To witness your gaze of excitement
As the energy in your little body swells
And squeals come from your mouth.

A caterpillar,
Snow,
Ferris wheels,
Puppies,
Animals,
And more.

All get the same reaction
as your sense of wonder of the world around you
fills every space.
A gift to witness
when in the presence of your grace.

Will it be Okay?

Today, when things are like this.
When it's a little harder to breathe
Because it feels like a massive weight is on my
chest as panic has filled every space of my body.
Today, when things are like this
I need to know…

Will it be okay?
Will I survive the waves of life that keep
crashing down?
As the wind swirls around the millions of
thoughts in my head
I wonder if this new medication will help
provide some reprieve for the chaos of my soul.
Will it be okay?
I need to know.
Especially when things are like this causing me
to wonder
Can I hold on?

Intimacy

Before you, intimacy wasn't safe.
It was like engaging in acts without consent ever since my voice was taken and I separated from the core of my body long ago.

Before you, it was complete detachment within multiple castles set upon a labyrinth of lock rooms, winding halls, and levels with no direction.
But, no one knew.
Until, you.

One by one,
Step by step,
Forward, backward
We went so slow.
Safety was built from scratch with no pressure from any side.
Intimacy was created from the beginning of the moment we took a chance and allowed us to have our guard down within the safety that was us.

Discovering touch.
Deep connection.

Sexual safety and attraction filled with love.
All while we traveled the labyrinth together with
the intimacy of our souls that have fully
embraced and loved each other.

Enough

When the doubt begins to creep in
And the voices rise from their sleep inside
Filling your mind, tightening your lungs,
puppeteering your tongue
As you grasp for anything to hold onto before
you fade into the darkness behind the voices of
your internal systems home estate;

I reach my hand out and say:

I got you.
I see you.
I hear you.
I feel you.
I know what they are saying right now as I lock
into your struggling gaze.
I want you to know.
I need you to know.
Hold on tight right here
My hand in yours as our souls connect
embracing deep into the power as I say…

You are enough.
I am enough.
We are enough.
Always.

Is It Real?

They said it wasn't possible.
It just doesn't exist said with such frustration
and annoyance.
Why can't you just settle?
Why can't you just fit?
We are offering you healing…

Healing from sexual assaults
Healing from trauma
Healing from hate
Healing from homelessness
Healing from everything
That has happened
That is happening to you.

We are offering you a chance to be fixed once
and for all.
On our terms.

Just sign your soul on the dotted line.
Here. Right Here.
Wait, why are you walking away?
This is the best you will ever get.
We can help you here.

They said it wasn't possible.
They covered up my voice and my experience
with their terms.
They tried to make me into something else by
calling it healing.
But, now I know.
They were wrong.
They retraumatize.
They tried to keep me from discovering my true
worth.

They lost.
I won.
Is it real?
Yes, I am on the journey to discovering who I
truly am within all my trauma and glory.
They lost.
I won.

Wild Laughter

The infectious sound comes from deep inside
your belly
Filling your lungs and traveling through the air.
It spreads like wild laughter with no container
by any means.

One, two, three.
We join you as the wild laughter causes us to let
go of everything.
Work, stress, money, bills, health.
The list goes on.
In just a moment
Time stops,
Wild laughter grounding us all into the present
moment with each other.

Pick Up Your Feet!

It sounds simple.
"Pick up your feet"
As to insinuate I can prevent my falls.
Do they have spasticity?
Do they know what it feels like to have legs
like metal pipes being twisted, stretched, curled?
How would the pipe feel if you were trying to do
that with it?
How would you feel after putting all your
mighty strength into it and yet it won't budge?
What would you say?
How would you feel?

It's not easy living with spasticity.
It hurts every second of everyday with no
escape.
I wish I could pick up my feet as easily as you
make it sound.
I wish I could take the pain away.

The dream of what it would be like to live a day
without physical pain while
Getting dressed,
Playing with my friends,
Working,

Parenting,
Bathing,
Eating,
Living.

I can pick up my feet no more now at almost 40
than I could at 5.
So to every voice and every thought,
Please know,
It's called spasticity and I don't have control
over picking up my feet.

Stigma

Stigma.
Keeps others from getting to know me.
Stigma.
Keeps me from getting to know myself.
Stigma.
Puts up walls within relationships.
Stigma.
Broke up my family.
Stigma.
Kept me from getting the help I so desperately
was seeking.
Kept me from accessing the support I needed.
Stigma.
Told me I wasn't capable.
Stigma.
Created a false sense of identity.
Stigma.
It's at the core of so much advocacy work.
Yet.
Stigma keeps fracturing all the different parts of
me.
All are stigmatized in different ways.
Never able to be together as one in the same
space.

Only You

In the quiet of dusk
In the raging light of dawn
Only you see what's behind my eyes.

In the untouchable moments
Only you are let close enough.

In the traveling of roads with twists and turns
A locked door here and new wall there.
Only you have been given the sacred key to the
house down the twisted road with the labyrinth
of rooms and locked doors.

Only you get to see the me
Out in the open and behind closed doors.
Only you.

A Request: Paint me like I am

Paint me like I am
In all my glory
My fullness
My wholeness.
Paint the light
Paint the joy
Paint the hope
Paint the love
Paint all the colors of my soul
Paint my soul alive.
But don't forget to paint
The raw
The dark
The dirty
The hidden
The curves
The scars
The vulnerability
The authenticity
Of everything that I am
Because without including those things
Can you truly paint me like I am?
The both/and
I need to see it

I need to feel it
I need to accept it as it makes me who I am
In all my glory
My fullness
My wholeness of me.
Paint me like I am
In all the versions tethered as one
Making up the wholeness of me.
I need to see it
I want to know you can do it
I need to know we both won't cover up any part
of who I am,
who you are,
who we are together.

Thoughts from One to Another

Sometimes when I walk the world I wish you
knew me.
I also wish I knew me too.
Only memories plague my mind.

But, the memories don't tell me who I am or
whether I ever knew who I was.

It's just blank.
I am more than I see.
I am stronger than I think.

I am more knowledgeable and wise than I am
aware of.
While everyone wants money and fame,

I want freedom from the chains which hold me
captive to my own mind.

I want peace to fill my mind, body, and soul.
I want to be able to feel love and true happiness.
These are worth more than money and fame to
someone like me.

I am more than I see.
I am stronger than I think.

I am more knowledgeable and wise than I am
aware of.

You have a voice.
You are worth more than you think.
You deserve love.

You deserve to fully experience a full life.
You will believe in this one day too,

Until that day,
Leave it to me to show you.

Free

She looks in the mirror,
She hates everything about herself
Why can't she just make it all go away.
Things are so very hard
And so very confusing all the time
I wish SHE wasn't ME.
I feel like I'm always drowning
I feel like I am always screaming
But, no one else can hear.
No one except her
But her message cuts deep into the hope of my
soul
Child, you need to always remember your place
You are already tainted with the messages of
disgust.
You are:
Crippled,
Not dark enough
Not light enough either
Slow to understand
Different.
This world doesn't like different.
The world doesn't like the forbidden
Sex, queer, domestic violence, hardship, living
outside the lines

Don' tyou dare go there
For if you do,
You will lose EVERYTHING
.

Stay quiet and conform
Don't be difficult
Get married
Follow the traditional path
Make us proud
Only then will you be worthy, loved, good, and
safe.
My heart breaks
My soul weeps
Oh how messy, conflicted, and scary this life is.
I wish I wasn't so alone
I wish I was anything other than me.
I blamed myself every time my husband abused
me

I blamed myself for the sexual assaults
I blamed myself for all life's hardships that came
storming in as
Life grew very long.
I look into the mirror
As she looks back at me
I hear all the messages she carried, and the
thoughts that came along:
She deserved it
She wasn't quiet enough,

She didn't conform enough
She was an abomination, unworthy, unlovable, a
mistake
She struggled to follow the traditional roles and
paths to much
She wished she was never born
She WAS me.
I reach through the mirror
With a deep embrace
I hold her emotions
I hold her life
I gently whisper into her soul of tears
It's okay
To be queer,
To love and be loved
To be a man
To transition into the handsome man she knew
herself to be
It's okay
You are not alone anymore
I love you exactly as you are
You are free.

New

New
It doesn't seem to ever ask me
What I want;
What I think;
What I need.
I wonder if it knows how scary it is to me.
Yet, there are those times,
when I know in my heart the venture needs to be
made;
No matter how terribly frightening in my bones
it is to me.
So once again
The new is coming.
It is here.
It fills every space and void.
Deathly afraid;
I take a deep breath.
Braveness enters
Fear and the other emotions gather around
They hold hands.
They reach for mine;
And
Together we all step out
Into Uncertainty;
Into the unknown;
Capable of anything.

Believe

Believe
In a brand new day;
In the hope of tomorrow;
In that which might seem like an uphill battle is
indeed a battle,
A battle that will eventually break to the dawn of
something new;
In what might seem impossible, is indeed,
possible.
In the brand new day waiting for me.
Believe
In yourself;
Your vision;
Your worthiness;
Your awesomeness;
Your voice;
Your story;
Your hopes;
Your dreams;
Your abilities;
All that you already are;
And the person you aspire to be.

On the Journey to Me

It's a new day,
My suitcase is packed,
Just five things;
But, that's all I need.
Together we're about to embark on a journey;
A journey to me.

My Past;
It takes up a lot of room in the suitcase.
Sometimes the rest of us wonder why it is there.
Because there were good memories, I don't want
to forget.
To remain connected to my ancestors and their
stories.
To continue to heal and grow from it,
To let go of the shame we have from it.
And to remember,
I am strong and able to overcome and obstacle
that comes my way.
That's why my past has a place in the suitcase.
That is why we shook hands,
Knowing we had to take the journey together.

My lifelines.
Art,

Music,
Movies,
Natures,
Water,
Creativity,
Photographs,
Quality Time;
There was no question about it.
I wouldn't be today without them.
This journey needs them.
They are my helping breath and light along the
way.

My belief that I, myself, am sacred and holy;
A space in the suitcase connected to wonder and
desire.
Yes, Sacred;
Yes, Holy;
So, that I may value and prioritize
Self Care.
Self Love.
Kindness;
Gentleness;

Self Esteem.
My body;
All aspects of my being are held as nothing other
than holy.

I wonder what it would be like to reach the end
of this journey,
I wonder actually believe these things about me.
I wonder can I actually value and love myself.
Right now, it seems so far away
But, I believe it's possible because we are
already on our way.

Voice;
My voice;
Because I know what it's like to not have one.
To not be able to use it;
To not be heard when it is used;
I never want to go back there again.
A journey to me without my voice is not a
journey I want to take.
It is not a journey leading to me.
It is settled,
My voice is coming.
No negotiations.
Belief in a brand new day;
A belief that brings me
Hope,
Joy,
Possibility,
Chances,
Growth,
Self Discovery,
Connection,

Freedom,
And
A belief that led me on this journey to me.

Reflection of Myself

In the mirror's gaze, we often peer,
Reflecting on what we hold dear.
But self-image is more than meets the eye,
It's the essence within, reaching for the sky.

In every curve and line, a story unfolds,
The journey of life, the tales it holds.
Scars and imperfections, too play a part,
In the masterpiece of you, a work of art.

Embrace the uniqueness, the quirks you possess,
In self-acceptance, find happiness.
For beauty transcends the outward view,
It's the confidence and love that shine through.

Let not society's standards define your worth,
You're a gem, a treasure since your birth.
In the mirror, see strength, resilience, and grace,
A reflection of life's beautiful embrace.

Self-image, is a canvas where you can paint,
A portrait of love, free from restraint.
In your own eyes, find the love you seek,
Self-image begins with how you speak.

To yourself, with kindness and care,
Celebrate the beauty that's always there.
In the tapestry of life, you're a vibrant hue,
A masterpiece of self, forever true.